Protective Orders And Child Protective Orders

Useful Info That May Help You Protect Yourself Or Your Children Against Abuse (Or False Allegations Of Abuse) In Utah

Kelly Peterson, Esq.

ISBN: 978-1-941645-07-9

Designed and Published by:

Speakeasy Publications

73-03 Bell Blvd, #10
Oakland Gardens, NY 11364
www.SpeakeasyMarketingInc.com
888-225-8594

Disclaimer

This publication is intended to be informational only. No legal advice is being given, and no attorney-client relationship is intended to be created by reading this material. If you are facing legal issues, whether criminal or civil, seek professional legal counsel to get your questions answered.

Law Office of Kelly Peterson
2696 N University Ave.,
Suite 240 Provo, UT 84604
(801) 375-0484
www.kmpetersonlaw.net

Testimonials

"He is an extraordinary attorney, and stands out among the attorneys in this area. In my experience, Mr. Peterson has always been well prepared for any case in which he takes a position. He does his homework, meets with his clients, and is reasonable, as well as smart in his presentations to the court and to opposing counsel. It is a pleasure to work with him because I know he always has a factual and valid legal basis for the claims he makes. He never takes a case personally, but makes decisions based on objective criteria and good research. Further, he is personable and honest."

- Lori Fowlke, Local Attorney with over 20-Year Experience in Family Law

"Kelly has consistently proven himself to be a highly skilled litigator. His pre-trial preparation is among the most thorough that I have ever seen. What perhaps has been the most surprising aspect to me is how efficient his methods are. Time is not wasted, and quality work product is quickly produced. He has earned a reputation in the legal community as a strong, aggressive trial lawyer. Although he is always willing to work collaboratively toward mutually agreed case resolution, he is never afraid of engaging in the full battle, when necessary."

- F. Richards Smith, former director, Office of Guardian ad Litem

"I am impressed by Kelly's work ethic and efficiency. He works extremely hard and is always ultra-prepared for his court hearings and trials. He has refined his system of investigating and case preparation to be extremely efficient and effective. Kelly is respected by the local bar and judges, as being very competent, consistently prepared, exhibiting good judgment, and being a first rate trial lawyer. Kelly is considered to be among the most expert and proactive of district court Guardians ad Litem (GAL) attorneys in Utah. Kelly possesses integrity, honesty, civility, dependability, and professionalism. He has also demonstrated grace under pressure repeatedly. He has performed an outstanding job in a very difficult and high-conflict area of law."

- R. John Moody, Managing Attorney, Fourth District Office of Guardian ad Litem

"Kelly has a unique ability to see to the heart of complex issues, dispense with frivolous matters, and focus on what is important. He has strong analytical ability and argues persuasively. Kelly has an easy, thoughtful manner that makes him...easy to work with. However, when he makes up his mind on the right course of action, he defends that position with firmness and tenacity without being overbearing. Moreover, I have observed Kelly to be both honest and ethical."

- Judge (retired) Norman H. Jackson, Utah Court of Appeals, Previous Employer

"We consider him to have been a valuable asset to this firm. He has good judgment, integrity, and common sense. Further, Kelly is a skilled and capable advocate, both in transactional work and in litigation. He zealously represents his clients, but does so in a civil, professional manner, without the need to resort to posturing, intimidation, or similar tactics. We have also observed Kelly to be thorough, thoughtful, and detailed in all aspects of his practice. The foregoing qualities, together with a solid courtroom presence, have led Kelly to be well-liked and respected by the local bar and judges. Kelly engenders confidence in his clients, who find it easy to trust his judgment and advice. Most importantly, Kelly is dependable. There has not been one occasion where Kelly has failed to accomplish a task by the deadline, and the ability to depend on that trait makes him invaluable in our practice."

- Jeff Ouderkirk & Jeff Hollen, Previous Employers

"Kelly and I have had the privilege of working on many cases together. Through his diligence and dedication, lives were saved. Kelly is a thorough professional. Without question he is dedicated to his perception of the best interests of his clients. Kelly is decisive. He is not afraid to make a decision. I have observed him being confronted by hostile parties. In such circumstances I have always observed him to be calm, poised, and reflective. Kelly Peterson will continue to be a credit to the legal profession."

- Brent Young, Local Attorney with over 33-Year Experience in Family Law

"He is passionate in his representation of the children in his care. Kelly is thorough in his trial preparation. I do not believe there is an attorney in Fourth District who understands the Rules of Civil Procedure and Rules of Evidence better than Kelly. He spends the time to meet with his clients, parents and others to be able to make recommendations as to the best interests of the children. He is both determined and persistent in advocating for them. I know there are children who are alive and healthy today because of Kelly's willingness to go the extra mile. He will take a stand, and follow through with the steps necessary to get to a positive outcome. I have also seen Kelly serve as a very effective partner in mediations. He works with the parents in a thoughtful and kind manner. Kelly will be a wonderful asset."

- Sandra Dredge, Local Attorney with over 21-Year Experience in Family Law

TABLE OF CONTENTS

AUTHOR INTRODUCTION

Since 2002, the bulk of Kelly's practice has included complex family law matters. Over the years and in two different states, Kelly Peterson earned a reputation for effectively handling high-conflict matters involving such areas as complex financial issues, substance abuse, child abuse/neglect (and false allegations thereof), mental health issues, and domestic violence. He has effectively represented his clients in literally thousands of court hearings.

Additionally, Kelly has helped resolve hundreds of cases in mediation, has represented abused and neglected children as a Guardian ad Litem, and represented clients in a variety of other civil areas.

After obtaining his law degree at BYU in 2000, Kelly clerked at the Utah Court of Appeals allowing him to develop appellate-quality research and writing ability. These skills later proved essential to quality representation of his clients.

In 2010, Kelly underwent the rigorous certification process to become a Child Welfare Law Specialist (CWLS). Few private attorneys in Utah hold this distinction, which is obtained through the National Association of Counsel for Children (NACC).

Because of his expertise in these areas, attorneys and therapists have invited Kelly to be a guest lecturer on areas such as: defending against dirty litigation tactics, forensic interviewing of adults, and the handling of expert witnesses in court. Also, Kelly compiled an extensive legal reference guide for family law and juvenile court that is used state-wide by family law attorneys, juvenile court attorneys, mediators and judges.

When not at the office, Kelly spends as much time as possible with his lovely wife and hilarious children.

WHAT IS A PROTECTIVE ORDER IN UTAH?

In the state of Utah a protective order is in an order which is both criminal and civil in nature. If two parties have been cohabitants, meaning they were married, related by blood, have children in common, are the biological parent of an unborn child or they have resided in the same residence and there has been domestic violence then a protective order can be obtained.

The order gives the court discretion to keep the parties apart, where it becomes a crime if the respondent has any further contact with the petitioner other than what is set forth in the order. It can also order quite a number of things such as temporary child support, temporary custody or temporary visitation. Additionally, it can also order that a party doesn't have access to firearms and also issue similar orders. It comes down to what the petitioner asks for in the protective order petition.

In the State of Utah once an order has been issued, there are civil provisions and as well as criminal provisions. The criminal provisions are generally no contact provisions or there are limitations on the contact. Those do not go away without a court order. They are indefinite and if someone violates that provision that becomes a crime. All the petitioner then has to do is call law enforcement, advise that there has been a protective order violation of the criminal provisions. Police can then arrest or cite the violator. The civil provisions, on the other hand, relate to matters including temporary custody, temporary visitation and temporary child support. If those provisions are violated, that would not be considered a crime.

Protective orders can award custody, visitation, child support or temporary possession of a home. In order to have the other party sanctioned for a civil provision, you would have to file a motion in a civil court. The criminal provisions obviously last much longer whereas, the civil provisions generally expire after 150 days, unless specifically extended by the court. The civil provisions act as a band aid to give the petitioner time to file, whether it be a divorce petition or a custody petition, and to get temporary orders in place in that new custody case.

Often, it can take time to get temporary orders in place, and so this is a method of obtaining orders very quickly for a short term basis until you can get into the proper court on those civil provisions.

How Is A Restraining Order Different From A Protective Order?

In the vocabulary of Utah courts, a restraining order is civil in nature. Usually a restraining order is an order in a divorce, custody case, or paternity case that restrains the contact of the parties. For example, even if a protective order is not in place there can be civil restraining orders in a divorce or a paternity case that prohibit the parties from contacting each other except in certain ways. It prohibits each other from dissipating marital assets, or from disparaging the other party in front of the children, or any other behavior that the court believes needs to be restrained.

Again, it is civil in nature so to enforce it you have to file what is known as an order to show cause to have the other party sanctioned. Unlike under criminal provisions, you can't call the police and tell them there has been a violation in the civil restraining order. Again, it is not a crime to violate a civil restraining order even though it might be in contempt to do so. The main difference between a restraining order and a protective order are the remedies for enforcement. In a protective order you can call law enforcement, at least for the criminal provisions, whereas by definition the restraining order in Utah is going to be civil in nature, so you have to file an order to show cause instead.

TYPES OF PROTECTIVE ORDERS

There are two types of protective orders; adult protective orders and child protective orders. Any interested party can file a petition for a child protective order to prohibit someone from having contact with a child. In Utah the grounds for obtaining a child protective order, is that you have to show physical abuse, sexual abuse, or imminent threat thereof to the child. These orders are criminal in nature, which means if violated law enforcement can step in.

What Is The Criteria For A Protection Order To Be Put Into Place?

For a protection order to be put into place, the two parties have to be cohabitants, and the Cohabitant Abuse Act is Utah Code Annotated 78B–7–101. Section 102 defines a cohabitant as someone who is 16 years of age or older who is or was a spouse, is related by blood or marriage, has had one or more children in common with the other party, is the biological parent of an unborn child, or resides or has resided in the same

residence as the other party. That is the first element that needs to be met. The next element that needs to be met is there has to be domestic violence, and domestic violence is also defined in sub section, 102, which refers to a different statute. It is any criminal offense involving violence of physical harm or threat of violence or physical harm, or any threat, conspiracy, or solicitation to commit a criminal offense involving violence or physical harm when committed by one cohabitant against another. It also means the commission or attempt to commit any of the following offenses against the other: assault, aggravated assault, homicide, harassment, electronic communications harassment, kidnapping, mayhem, sexual offenses, stalking, unlawful detention, and violation of a protective order and even if it is a temporary protective order is also grounds for the entry of a protective order.

Certain offenses against property are also included such as: destruction of property or burglary, criminal trespass, robbery, possession of a deadly weapon with intent to assault, discharge of a firearm, disorderly conduct in certain cases, and child abuse.

All of these things are considered to be domestic violence in addition to the general definition. If those two things are found, that someone is a cohabitant and domestic violence has occurred, then generally a protective order will be issued.

How Often Are Protective Orders Involved In Divorce Situations?

Very often a protective order will precede a divorce or custody action, or will follow shortly on the heels of a paternity or divorce filing. The legitimate reasons this tends to happen might be if there was domestic violence involved and now one party needs protection from the other. That often coincides with their irreconcilable differences that are going to precede the divorce. However, the protective order process can be abused by people simply trying to get a leg up in the current or anticipated divorce litigation or custody litigation. By alleging domestic violence occurred when it didn't really happen, one party may be attempting to

get temporary possession of the residence, temporary custody of the children, or temporary supervision of the other party's parenting time.

A protective order can also sometimes force separation instantly. Let's suppose, for example, that two people are living in a home and have decided to get a divorce but neither is willing to leave. There are often times where one party may falsely allege domestic violence in order to force the removal of the other person from the home. This could potentially also force a quick order of temporary custody so that the accuser has an advantage in an upcoming custody dispute.

What Is Considered A Violation Of Protective Order?

If someone violates the criminal provisions of a protective order the petitioner can contact law enforcement. Police may either cite the violator or even make an arrest and take him or her immediately to a general pending bail hearing if there is sufficient evidence or probable cause that the order was violated. As for violations against the civil provisions of a protective order, the petitioner would have to file an order to show cause against the alleged accused.

However, just because you have the option of calling law enforcement to help enforce the protective order, that doesn't mean you can't file an order to show cause for someone violating the civil provisions of the protective order as well. You can do both. However, most of the time people would rather have law enforcement do the work for them, being a more immediate result and could possibly result in instant incarceration.

HOW ARE PROTECTIVE ORDERS FILED?

A protective order is initiated by one party filing a protective order petition, which must be done using specific state approved forms which can be obtained online. There is also usually a victim's advocate either at the police station or at the courthouse who can assist. Along with the petition, an ex parte, or a temporary order, is then submitted. The purpose of the ex parte order is to ask the judge to ensure the other side will not know that this is being submitted, with the understanding that we will have a hearing very soon. Under Utah law, the hearing must take place within 20 days of the issuance of the ex parte or the temporary order, and it is to see if the order is going to remain in place permanently. Once the attorney, victim's advocate or person themselves will submit to the court a protective order petition and proposed order. There is no fee and it will immediately be given to a judge.

The judge will then review the facts in the petition, determine if the parties are cohabitants, and ask him or herself, “If the allegations contained herein are true, do they meet the requirements set forth in the statute for a protective order?” If the answer is yes, the judge will then sign the ex parte or the temporary protective order, and it will be uploaded to the law enforcement system.

Law enforcement will then be directed to serve the order on the other party. In the ex parte or the temporary protective order there will be a date and a time for the respondent to show up at a hearing, at which point the petitioner is going to have to prove, by a preponderance of the evidence (which is essentially 51% of the evidence or more) that they are cohabitants and that the domestic violence occurred.

If at that hearing they are able to meet that criteria, then a permanent protective order will enter. If the respondent does not show up for the hearing and the petitioner does, then the petitioner will be entitled to a default and will win automatically, assuming that the respondent has been properly served.

On the other hand, if the respondent shows up and the petitioner does not, then the order will automatically be dismissed.

Can A Protective Order Be Modified Or Dismissed?

If both parties agree, then a protective order can be changed and the court can enter a modified protective order. However, the court on its own authority can also modify the protective order if there is sufficient reason and evidence to do so. For example, if the involved parties are having a hearing in a divorce or custody manner, and evidence is presented to the judge that shows the protective order ought to be modified, the court on its own authority can do so.

The Impact Of Having A Protective Order Placed Against You

Having a protective order placed against you means it will show up as part of your criminal record. That can impact many areas of a person's life including potentially scaring away potential employers who run a background check, for example. Additionally under federal guidelines someone who has a protective order against him or her cannot possess firearms.

Additionally if someone is an immigrant, then a protective order can be a very serious issue as it may negatively impact their ability to be naturalized, or they might have their immigration status revoked.

How Long Does A Protection Order Last In Utah?

The initial temporary protective order expires at the date and time that the hearing is set. For example, if the hearing is set 15 days from now at a certain date and time, that is when it expires. The court can extend the temporary protective order under a number of circumstances. For example, one reason may be that the respondent hasn't been properly served. Another example may be if the parties are attempting to reach a settlement and now don't want a permanent protective order but the petitioner is unable to give up the temporary protective order. It is possible they can stipulate to extending the protective order and setting a new hearing date while they're trying to work things out.

Once a permanent protective order is entered it is indefinite unless it is dismissed by a court. Subsection 113 refers to the dismissal of a protective order and gives various methods by which that can be done. One way is if the protective order has been in effect for at least two years and the court determines the petitioner no longer has a reasonable fear of future abuse, the court can dismiss the order. Additionally after the order of protection has been in place for several years, the respondent can request a hearing to demonstrate that the protective order is no longer needed and the petitioner no longer has a reasonable fear. The court also can amend or dismiss a protective order that has been in effect for at least one year if it finds that the reason for the issuance of the protective order no longer exists, or if the petitioner has repeatedly acted in contravention to the protective order.

For example, a protective order restrains the respondent from contacting the petitioner, but it does not restrain the petitioner from contacting a respondent. If the petitioner is repeatedly contacting the respondent after the order is issued or is knowingly is trying to induce the respondent to communicate so that he commits a violation, the court may dismiss the order. Another example may be where the petitioner's actions demonstrate that the petitioner no longer has a reasonable fear. All of this, of course, presupposes that there have been no protective order violations.

If there have been any violations, the court cannot dismiss the protective order. If there is a divorce pending then when the divorce decree enters, the court has the discretion to dismiss the protective order at the same time. Additionally a protective order will expire automatically 10 years from the date of the entry of a divorce decree, or 10 years from the date of the entry of the protective order.

What Is A Child Protective Order?

Similar to an adult protective order, it is a court order that has both civil and criminal provisions, usually restraining somebody from having contact with the child if they are not a parent or from having unsupervised contact (or in some way limiting the contact between a child and the respondent if the respondent is a parent). It is a creature of statute, meaning that there is no common law right to a protective order, either adult or child protective order. The scope and limits of what you can obtain with a child protective order is set forth in the statutes.

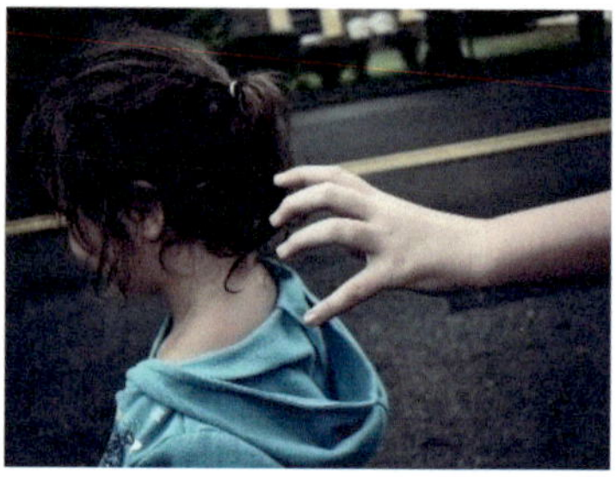

How Do Child Protective Orders Differ From Adult Protective Orders?

There are a couple of ways that protective orders differ from child to adult. First, obviously they are protecting a child instead of an adult. With an adult protective order, the person who files the protective order must be the adult who wants the protection. You cannot file an adult protective order on behalf of someone else. With the child protective order, any “interested person,” who is almost anybody that has some legitimate connection with the child, may file a petition on behalf of a child. A court can place a protective order for a child case, but it is more limited.

An adult protective order has more expansive additional relief that you can request. For example, return of property, and child support to name a few. Another important difference between an adult protective order and a child is the grounds upon which a protective order can be granted. We have discussed above the grounds for obtaining an adult protective order that surrounds domestic violence. In order to obtain an adult protective order, there are numerous ways of demonstrating some kind of domestic violence to obtain an adult protective order. But in a child protective order in the state of Utah, you have to show that the child has been abused or are at imminent risk of being in danger.

The term “Abuse” in the child protective order statute is defined very narrowly. In other places in the code and in case law, child abuse can be defined much more expansively, but under the definitions of the child protective order statute, it is defined as physical abuse, sexual abuse or imminent risk thereof.

The definition allows for a bit of leg room to expand it more slightly broadly than physical or sexual abuse, but not much. Occasionally, a court may define imminent risk of physical or sexual abuse to include failure to protect by somebody who should be protecting the child, usually a parent or a grandparent. For example, suppose that there is a parent who is married to a pedophile, or a parent is married or cohabiting with somebody who is abusing the child. Even though the parent themselves are not the ones perpetrating on the child physically or sexually, if they have a knowledge that it is likely to occur, and yet they still continue to expose the child to that environment, then a child protective order can also enter against the parent who is failing to protect. This is an extreme example, but it illustrates the point, the failure to protect on occasion if it is very clear that the respondent in the protective order is knowingly putting the child in a situation where they are likely to suffer physical, sexual abuse or extreme emotional harm to the point where it is going to stunt them developmentally. Then a child protective order could be entered against them.

How Common Is It For The Court To Deny A Child Protective Order?

It is not uncommon that the party requesting a child protective order does not really know how to go about it. For example if a parent is concerned that the other parent has a drug habit, they can file a child protective order because the other parent is addicted to drugs and could cause harm to the child. Very often the court will deny even the initial temporary protective order because it fails to meet the narrow definition of abuse under the statute, which essentially is physical or sexual abuse, and imminent risk thereof.

There is alienation, emotional abuse, and many other types of abuses that are not covered in the definition of abuse under the statute in our state. So the court will often deny a temporary protective order under those circumstances. If a child protective order is denied at the ex parte or temporary level, upon request of the petitioner, a hearing can be granted on that denial within twenty days after the denial.

The hearing will occur within twenty days of the denial upon request of the petitioner. I rarely have seen that happen, usually it is denied, because it fails to meet the definition of abuse. That is the most common scenario, and once the petitioner realize the problem, they will usually seek other avenues for relief.

What Is The Process Of Filing For A Child Protective Order?

The process of filing for a child protective order is similar to an adult protective order. A temporary protective order usually issues ex-parte, meaning both sides have not had an opportunity to argue before the judge before it enters. Once someone files a petition for the entry of a child protective order, they also submit a proposed temporary protective order for the court to sign. If the court believes that there is jurisdiction and that the allegations in the petition satisfies the definitions of abuse, then the court can issue a temporary protective order which will then go out to law enforcement and will be served on the respondent. The temporary protective order expires after twenty days, or whenever the hearing is scheduled, whichever occurs first.

The court is required to schedule a hearing within those twenty days upon entry of the temporary protective order. Once the respondent is served with the temporary protective order, they will have notice of the date and time of the hearing, and they must show up to defend themselves. Depending on whether you are in a metropolitan or a rural area in the state of Utah, you may have either a court commissioner or a judge who will hear the case. A court commissioner does not have the broad expanse of powers that a judge has. They have a certain amount of judicial authority to hear matters on a temporary basis.

If the matter is heard before a court commissioner, then likely no evidence will be taken. This means that the court will decide the issue based on proffer and a proffer would occur when let us say the attorney for the petitioner would stand up and say, "Your Honor, here is my client. His or her name is so and so, and if called to testify today, she would state following. She has brought with her the following witnesses, and if called to testify, this is what they would say". Then the respondent's attorney would get up and say, "Here is my client, his or her name is so and so and if called to testify, here's what he or she would say and here are his or her witnesses and if called to testify, this is what they would say", and the commissioner would make a determination about whether or not there are grounds for entry of a child protective order.

If the matter is being heard before a judge, then the judge can choose to have a proffer hearing, like the one described above, or the court can choose to take evidence, meaning that witness by witness, they will each be put on the stand, examined and cross-examined. If a proffer hearing is held before a commissioner, and either side wishes to object to the commissioner's ruling, they are allowed to file an objection within fourteen days after the commissioner enters his or her ruling. At that point, the judge can schedule a hearing and may choose to hear the matter with fresh eyes. If a protective order enters, then usually the court will sign the protective order in the presence of the respondent and serve them with the copy of it right in court. It is in effect at that moment. If the respondent

violates the terms of the child protective order, then they can be arrested.

When Is A Guardian Ad Litem Appointed In This Scenario?

In the state of Utah, Guardian ad Litems are not just laypeople. They are attorneys who are the voice for the children and they represent the children. The court has the discretion to appoint a Guardian ad Litem on any case where abuse or neglect has been alleged. On rare occasions, a court declines to appoint a "GAL" in a child protective order matter, but most of the time, they will appoint an attorney guardian ad litem.

What Role Do Evidence Or Witnesses Play In Obtaining A Child Protective Order?

The same rule of evidence that applies in any civil matter also applies in protective orders. There are certain additional rules in juvenile court. Juvenile court has the authority to refer child protective orders to the district court. The district court is the court of general jurisdiction in Utah where divorces, paternity actions, custody actions and those kinds of things take place. Juvenile court does not hear these actions. The district court cannot refer a child protective order to the juvenile court, but the juvenile court has the authority to refer the matter over to the district court if there is a proceeding in a district court that might impact or be impacted by the protective order matter.

For example, if there is a custody case in district court, and one party to that custody case files a request for a protective order in the juvenile court system, the juvenile court will look and see if there is something in the district court and say, "Let's have one judge hear everything, so we don't risk two judges making different rulings regarding the best interest of the child". But otherwise, the usual rules of evidence apply, and it is extremely important to make sure the evidence is presented in the right way, is admissible, and witness testimonies appear in the court in the appropriate way.

If the matter is being heard before a commissioner, then there one rule allows witness statements to be submitted by an affidavit or declaration rather than having those people in the courtroom. But if a judge is presiding over the hearing, that rule does not apply and your witnesses must be in the courtroom and ready to testify. Without having the necessary evidence at the hearing, the court will likely find that the petitioner failed to meet his or her burden of proof, and allow the ex parte or temporary protective order to expire and the matter will be dismissed.

WHAT SPECIFICS DOES A CHILD PROTECTIVE ORDER INCLUDE?

A child protective order generally says whatever the court orders. But there is this statute 78B-7-204 that indicates what the court is allowed to order. It is considered a Class A misdemeanor to violate the protective order. The protective order may prohibit the respondent from threatening to commit or committing abuse of the minor child. They prohibit the respondent from harassing, telephoning, contacting or communicating with the minor directly or indirectly. They prohibit the respondent from entering or remaining upon the resident school or place of employment with the minor and the premises of any specified place. That is any place that was specified in the petition as being frequented by the child.

If the court finds that the use or a possession of a weapon poses the threat, then they can be prohibited from purchasing, using or possessing a firearm or any other specified type of weapon. The order can demand certain items of personal property of the child to be provided to the petitioner for the benefit of the child. It can determine on a temporary basis, custody, visitation, and determine child support. That is the extent of what a child protective order is allowed to do.

What If Someone Violates A Protective Order Thinking That It Is In The Best Interests Of A Child?

Suppose you have a child with your ex-spouse and now you are remarried and your ex-spouse believes that your new spouse has physically or sexually abused your child. They file a child protective order against your new spouse. What are you required to do? First of all, the child protective order restrains the respondent only, not other people. In other words, under those circumstances, you (as the spouse) are not under the jurisdiction of the court and are not ordered to do anything.

You cannot be arrested or charged with a crime for failure to comply with the child protective order if you are not the respondent in that protective order.

That said it would be a poor decision not to comply with the terms of the child protective order (e.g. allow your spouse knowingly to violate the child protective order). Doing so may generate grounds for your ex-spouse to start filing motions in the custody case describing how you, despite knowing that there was a child protective order in place, allowed contact between the child and the respondent in the child protective order, thereby giving rise to an argument that you are failing to protect the child from potential harm from your new spouse.

If you fail to adhere to it yourself, you are opening the door to further litigation against you. Also your spouse in that situation would likely be criminally liable and could possibly be arrested. The best thing to do is to encourage your spouse to comply with the child protective order until the hearing is resolved in a way that the restrictions caused by it are reduced or eliminated prudently.

How Can I Remedy The Situation If There Is A Protective Order Against Me?

If you are served with a petition and a temporary protective order, obviously the best thing to do is hire an attorney who is experienced in handling child protective orders to defend you so the protective order does not become permanent.

If it does become permanent, typically it is interpreted to last up to one-hundred and fifty days. Interestingly, the statutory form of the child protective order makes it seem like it is going to be longer than that. But the courts often interpret it to mean that it is going to expire in one-hundred and fifty days.

The child protective order though is supposed to include a statement about when the order expires, so it is really up to the judge to determine when it expires. If one spouse is filing a child protective order against the other parent, then the court will often have it expire either A) as soon as the issue can be heard in the custody court and district court; or B) within one-hundred and fifty days whichever occurs first. But the court does not have to do that. The court can extend it until the child's eighteenth birthday if it wishes. For example, the respondent in a child protective order is, say, a sex offender that really has no interest in ever seeing the child again, the court will likely extend the protective order to the child's eighteenth birthday, because the person has no interest in seeing the child ever again. However, if the respondent is a close relative or a parent, the court might have the child protective order expire sooner.

If you are the respondent in a protective order matter, hire an attorney, and defend yourself as vigorously as possible. That may require negotiation. For example, if the allegations against you is true and the other side has excellent evidence that they are true, then sometimes the best negotiating tactic is to submit voluntarily to the child protective order in exchange for concessions regarding how and when it will be removed. For example, if you agree to get into treatment/therapy and successfully complete it, at that point, it can be dismissed. However, if the allegations are false, then obtaining an attorney and vigorously defending yourself against it is the best plan of action.

How does one defend themselves in a protective order matter? If the allegations are false, the answer is usually to make use of the rules of evidence, forcing the other side to actually meet their burden of proof. They must show up with their witnesses that are going to testify on their behalf, and objecting to evidence that is inadmissible. Assuming the allegations are false, then the great likelihood is that the other side will be unable to meet their burden of proof if the respondent is defended by competent counsel.

Can A Child Protective Order Be Amended Or Removed?

Yes, you can file a motion to amend or remove a child protective order. But the provisions regarding removal of a protective order or dismissal, regarding the statutes, are less. In an adult protective order, the statute regarding amending or dismissing it, spells out very clearly that it must be done. The child protective order statute does not. The court will likely determine that it has the discretion to amend the child protective order for good cause shown, but the process for getting it dismissed is much less clear. It will probably be because once the court has determined grounds for the entry of a protective order and it is present, it sets the date by which it will expire.

Then the courts rule on when it will expire. It is ruled that this is the date it will be dismissed in advance. So the best tactic there would be to file a motion to amend the expiration date of the child protective order and ask the court to amend the previous ruling as to when it would expire.

Does A Judge Decide If The Protective Order Is To Be Amended Or Dismissed Or Can The Parent Have A Say In It?

The petitioner, who obtains the child protective order, can stipulate, or in other words agree, to removal of the child protective order. If they do, then each side signs a stipulation and a proposed order dismissing a protective order to the court. If both sides agree, the court will generally sign it as well. In fact, any respondent in a protective order should be very wary of any offer by the petitioner or anybody else to allow contact between themselves and the child unless the protective order has formally been dismissed.

A child protective order may allow limited contact with the child under some circumstances (e.g. supervised visitation). Let us suppose that the petitioner in the protective order offers to say, “We don’t need supervision anymore; let’s just give you a parent time or contact with the child without a supervisor present”, the respondent should not do so, because it is still technically a crime. On a number of occasions I have witnessed attempts by a petitioner to lure the respondent into making that mistake and then calling the police to have them arrested for violation of the protective order.

How Do You Help Clients To Focus In A Child Protective Order Scenario?

If it has reached the point where the child has been abused, neglected or they are abused physically or sexually or where they are defending themselves against those allegations, the motivation is inherently there. I do not necessarily have to motivate them to move in the right direction. What I do instead rather is to give them instructions, to first identify, short term goals; long term goals, if use of a child protective order makes sense.

I give them instructions on what evidence to gather, how to gather it, and what timeframes are needed and step by step directions as to what to do to either get the protective order instituted and to prepare for the protective order hearing in the case if I am representing a petitioner. If I am representing the respondent, then we discuss how to prepare for the hearing in order to defend themselves against the allegations, if the allegations are false. But if the allegations are true, I will often engage in negotiations with the other side to help satisfy the petitioner's concerns, and work with my client to sort out those concerns for any need for supervision or limited contact as quickly as possible, in a way that is advantageous to the respondent.

It is mainly just a step by step instruction. I help draft pleadings, prepare witnesses, and prepare parties for re-examination and cross-examination. If the case cannot be resolved, then we will go through the litigation process.

Can Someone Handle A Child Protective Order Case Without An Experienced Family Law Attorney?

Many times I have witnessed people handle a protective order without proper representation. It happens all the time. They make the attempt, but they are severely disadvantaged if they do not have an experienced family law attorney to support them. Oftentimes the results that they are seeking do not come to fruition because they lack of knowledge of how to proceed with the case. It is highly recommended that an experienced family law attorney that is specifically experienced in handling child protective orders and is familiar with both district court and juvenile court be on hand to assist.

Parent Respondents Should Have As Much Contact With Their Child As Possible

If you are a parent of the child, and you have a child protective order against you, don't say to yourself: "Fine. I'm just not going to see the child. When the child wants

to see me, maybe I'll wait six months till this is dismissed or 5 months or whatever." That is a bad idea because there is case law in the state of Utah that say that unless you do everything that you can to resolve a child protective order and to have as much contact with your child as possible, even though there is a child protective order in place, you might be considered to be abandoning your child.

Abandonment is grounds for termination of your parental rights in our state.

If you have a protective order against you, you should do everything you can to get it removed either by engaging in the treatment necessary, and complying with any medical recommendations from any evaluator. For example, if it is physical abuse and the respondent has an anger problem, then they should enter in to an anger management program. If it is a domestic violence evaluation, then comply with the treatment recommendations, and then show up to the court with those treatment recommendations saying, "Look, I've done this. Can we amend the protective order to allow me to have more contact?"

In the meantime, whenever contact is allowed, that should be taken advantage of. But from time to time, I see a respondent who gets disgusted that there is a protective order against them and decides to punish the other party or punish the child passively by choosing to have no contact with the child. It can create grounds for abandonment, and I have seen parental rights terminated for that reason.

DISCLAIMER

This publication is intended to be informational only. No legal advice is being given, and no attorney-client relationship is intended to be created by reading this material. If you are facing legal issues, whether criminal or civil, seek professional legal counsel to get your questions answered.

Law Office of Kelly Peterson
(801) 375-0484
www.kmpetersonlaw.net

Made in the USA
Monee, IL
05 November 2026

67386578R00033